To my knowledge, Live To Dance, has been instrumental in educating six women to receive immediate medical treatment for heart problems which most likely saved their lives.

Ellen S. Abramson
author of Live To Dance

Fortunately, I was one of those six people.

October 13, 2013, I went to listen to Ellen Abramson, cardiac arrest survivor and author of Live to Dance, speak about heart health. I had been experiencing heart burn for the previous two days. Ellen mentioned that she also had heart burn before her heart attack. I began to get concerned. I went to lunch after her talk and sure enough I had heart burn again. I decided to call my doctor and was advised to call 911 immediately. After calling 911, I followed Ellen's advice and laid down by the unlocked door in case I passed out. To my shock, I had a heart attack and needed a stent. Without understanding that heart burn could be an indication of a heart attack, I would have never called my doctor or gone to the hospital. Without hearing Ellen's talk, my outcome may have been very different.

Kathy Nolte
heart attack survivor
St. Louis, Missouri

REVIEWS

"Important for every woman to read!

I read this book cover to cover the moment I got it in my hands. Her story is moving and touching and, for anyone who has ever had a heart attack or witnessed a loved one have one, it's deeply real and true. Her facts on this disease are given in a straight forward manner, skip all the medical terms. 1 in 3 women die from heart disease, and it's preventable with just simple changes. Her tips for preventing this disease are given in a realistic and honest way that is actually attainable and easily measurable. This book is clear, concise and real. Its real life, it really can happen to anyone, and there are very real ways to prevent it. If you love someone, share this book with them. It could make the difference in how long you get to have them here with you."

-YvonneSTL

"Thank you Ellen for sharing your remarkable story with us. It is both heart warming and informative. I've re-read it many times as there is much to digest . . I realized that as a woman, I did not know the signs of a heart attack. Yet, when my husband had his heart attack, I knew all the signs.

There is an old biblical quote that reads "To save one life is to save the world". I wonder how many lives your book can save!!!!!!"

-Florine Mamroth

"Inspiration for a healthier lifestyle.

I think the story of Elle's cardiac arrest and recovery should be a wake up call for women. We need to be more aware of the risks we face and the warning signs we may get. The book has very practical advice on how you can increase the chances you'll be around to dance, or do whatever else brings you joy!"

-Carol Holthouse (Wildwood, MO USA)

"Such an inspiring, life-changing story!

What a beautiful story! The letters your children wrote are priceless!!! I laughed and I cried. I enjoyed your bits of humor, but I was touched by the "realness" of your pain - both physical and emotional. You are such an inspiration for all women. Thank you for sharing your experience and thank you for being such a strong voice. YOU ARE A ROCK STAR!!!!

This book shares a real personal experience of cardiac arrest and how you can make simple changes in your life to lower your risk of heart disease and keep from suffering the same fate. A woman's greatest risk of death is from heart disease. Not only does this book help women recognize symptoms of a heart attack, but it also includes lifestyle and healthy eating tips to get you on the road to a healthier life. There are great journal sheets and worksheets along with the steps you need to take to get you on your way.

I'm so glad I read this book. I have a history of heart disease in my family. Mrs. Abramson's story will always stick with me. It has opened my eyes and made me aware that this just isn't a "man's" disease. This should be a must-read for all women. Knowledge is power and trust me.... you will get that from this book!"

-Wendi Lucchesi (Maryland Heights, Missouri United States)

"*The Life You Save May Be Your Own.*

Talking about heart health, especially to someone who doesn't want to hear what you have to say is never easy. They might not want yet another person telling them about their smoking habit, unhealthy weight or lack of exercise. If you never tell that person that you love them and want them to actually LIVE their life, you're doing them no favors.

Whether you need a pep talk, need to be reminded of the reasons to make healthy choices or enjoy inspirational stories from strong women, this book is for you. It might be something that you leave on someone's desk. You could give it to a friend who has survived a heart trauma to let her know that she's not alone. If you know someone fighting to win back their good health through proper diet and exercise, it could be the encouragement they need to keep trying.

The author tells a courageous story and shares valuable and potentially lifesaving information in an easy-to-read style. She makes you feel like you've just had lunch with a friend. It gives the wisdom of a medical journal with the warmth of a close girlfriend telling you about her life.

If you know someone who needs a wakeup call, pep talk or just to know that you care, this book would make a wonderful gift. The author does many speaking engagements and she is as informative as she is inspiring. Keep fighting for your good health and may you truly LIVE all the days of your life!"

-M. Langston (St. Louis, MO)

"*This is an amazing little book! Ellen not only tells her story in a funny, touching manner, but draws on the experiences of her family and friends as she went through the terrifying procedures to save her life. The background to the storyline is not overdone or pedantic, the event itself is captured with raw emotion. All women would be wise to heed Ellen's* words on the potentially deadly consequences of ignoring their own health issues. As a bonus, the book is filled with real-life examples and solutions to the often underreported issue of women and heart health."

-Robin L. Tidwell (St. Louis, MO)

"A riveting book that will change your life!

I purchased this book thinking it would be like all weight loss books, however I could not believe the impact it had on me. It is life-changing and will help you to see what your own life is about. Her account of her heart attack brought me to tears, however will change my life forever. For every woman who values her life, this book is a must read (especially if you have children). I will read this over and over to make sure I don't forget how important I am to myself and others. WOW we need more authors like Ellen."

-Jill Turec

Live to Dance

A Survivor's Story

Ellen S. Abramson

A Second Edition

authorHOUSE®

AuthorHouse™ *LLC*
1663 Liberty Drive
Bloomington, IN 47403
www.authorhouse.com
Phone: 1-800-839-8640

© 2012, 2014 Ellen S. Abramson. All rights reserved.

No part of this book may be reproduced, stored in a retrieval system, or transmitted by any means without the written permission of the author.

Published by AuthorHouse 01/24/2014

ISBN: 978-1-4670-4509-4 (sc)
ISBN: 978-1-4670-4510-0 (hc)
ISBN: 978-1-4670-4508-7 (e)

Library of Congress Control Number: 2011917871

Any people depicted in stock imagery provided by Thinkstock are models, and such images are being used for illustrative purposes only.
Certain stock imagery © Thinkstock.

This book is printed on acid-free paper.

Because of the dynamic nature of the Internet, any web addresses or links contained in this book may have changed since publication and may no longer be valid. The views expressed in this work are solely those of the author and do not necessarily reflect the views of the publisher, and the publisher hereby disclaims any responsibility for them.

I would like to dedicate this book to the One who allowed me to dance at my daughter's wedding and to celebrate each and every day of my life!

CONTENTS

Part One

Chapter 1 - Just Another Day in the Emergency Department by Dr. G.J. Beirne 3
Chapter 2 - Who Am I? 7
Chapter 3 - Why Write a Book? 9
Chapter 4 - My Story 13
Chapter 5 - My Husband's Perspective of What Happened On That Day 25
Chapter 6 - Intensive Care 27
Chapter 7 - It Took a Few Moments Of Death To Learn How To Live 29
Chapter 8 - Oprah Didn't Call and I Didn't Care 33
From My Daughter Heather 34
From My Son-in-Law Alan 36
From My Son Eric 37

Part Two

What Are You Willing To Do? 45
Chapter 9 - A Few Lines from Ralph Marston, a Favorite Poet of Mine 47
Chapter 10 - Heart Disease is Highly Preventable 49
Chapter 11 - Being Proactive 53
Chapter 12 - Act Quickly 55

Chapter 13 - Be Aware of the Warning Signs............ 57
Chapter 14 - Know Your Numbers 59
Healthy Weight Ranges... 60
Chapter 15 - The Two Things That I Did Right........... 61
Chapter 16 - How Do I Begin to Lose Weight?........... 65
Support 66
Clean Your Environment 67
Shop 67
Start Setting Goals 67
Have a Conversation with a Medical Doctor or
     Nutritionist... 68
Chapter 17 - Weight Loss Tips 71
Grocery Store 71
Dining Out... 72
Portion Control at Restaurants 73
Home 74
Portion Control at Home 74
General 75
Work 75
Friends and Family 76
Closet 76

Chapter 18 - Exercise 77
Exercise Benefits 77
Exercise Tips 79
Chapter 19 - Five Key Take-Aways From Your Local
    Cardiologist: 81

PART THREE

Your Workbook 85
Goals 88
Food & Exercise Journal 89
Action Steps 90
Action Steps for Week 1 91
Action Steps for Week 2 92
Action Steps for Week 3 93
Action Steps for Week 4 94
Action Steps for Week 5 95
Action Steps for Week 6 96

Acknowledgements

I'd like to thank all of my friends and family who showered me with love and attention when I needed it the most. Each and every one of you let me know that I am truly loved, especially at a time when I was in doubt. Family and friends were a big part of my healing process.

I also want to thank the doctors and staff at Missouri Baptist Hospital for enabling me to write this book. A special thanks to Dr. Greg Beirne and Dr. Greg Jones, Mary P., Maggie, and Registered Nurses Peg and Michelle for saving my life. Thank you to the Staff Cardiologist Dr. Groll, Chaplain Sherry Blankenship and Intensive Care Nurse Sonny for taking excellent care of me.

I want to thank Jan Breyer for inspiring me to write this book. A big shout out goes to my friends Lisa Marcus, and Carol Holthouse for providing me with the support and confidence I needed to make this happen.

I am appreciative of Dr. Pat Cole and Dr. Shari Cohen for giving me excellent health care. I know I am in good hands. Dr. Cole, thank you for the words "fit" and "thin" that you used to describe me. I cling to those words. Dr. Mauricio Sanchez and Dr. Amanda Hilmer Sanchez, thank you for saying that I do not look like someone who has survived cardiac arrest. Those words meant, and still mean, so much to me I worked very hard for the past two years to be healthy and dance at my daughter's wedding. What you expressed to me at the wedding rehearsal dinner put tears in my eyes. That's why I walked away. Thank you. I also would like to acknowledge my in-house cardiologist and son-in-law Alan. You have been so wonderful and patient with me. I love you and I am very proud, lucky and grateful to be your mother-in-law.

Part One

I have learned what your loved ones really want for their birthdays, weddings and graduations. They want to spend them with you.

Ellen Abramson

Chapter 1 - Just Another Day in the Emergency Department

By Dr. G.J. Beirne

Sunday, April 27, 2008, started out like any other day in the emergency department. I arrived for my triage shift, which began at 10 a.m. I typically arrive about 15-20 minutes before every shift to have some coffee, visit with my colleagues, and then sign onto the computer to access our electronic charting system. It was a beautiful, sunny spring day -- the kind of day when everything seems perfect.

At 10:08 a.m., a gentleman walked urgently into the ED and said "Can someone help me get my wife out of the car?" I went outside with him and found his wife in the back seat of the car. He told me her name was Ellen Abramson. She appeared quite pale and weak. Her husband told me she had been fine on waking that morning, but while working on the computer over the last 30-45 minutes, became very weak and felt sick. I lifted her out of the car and into a wheelchair and then wheeled her directly to the triage room. The triage nurse and I began our assessment, which typically is a brief review of medical, surgical and social history, home medications, and then a brief discussion of why the patient came to the emergency department. I enter orders for lab work, radiological studies, EKG, medications, etc, and the patient is then moved to a treatment room.

As an emergency medicine physician, one of our most valuable diagnostic tools is what is sometimes referred to as "clinical gestalt," or commonly called your "gut feeling." As I wheeled this woman into triage, I had the feeling that something was terribly wrong and that it was going to happen shortly. Ellen's pulse rate was about 40. When I asked her if it was normally this slow, she told me no. She was now more pale, sweaty and weak than just a few minutes ago, when I assisted her out of the car. At that point, we moved her to one of the emergency department treatment rooms for evaluation. An IV was started, she was placed on oxygen, and a 12-lead EKG was done. I continued to finish my brief evaluation as the triage physician in the room, then turned her care over to one of my colleagues.

The 12-lead EKG was done within a minute of arrival to the treatment room. It showed an inferior wall myocardial infarction ("heart attack") that was literally occurring at that moment. I yelled for our charge nurse to activate the cardiac cath lab team and get one of the cardiologists. Fortunately, one of the cardiologists was in the cardiac cath lab. While all of this "orchestrated chaos!" was occurring, I advised Ellen and her husband of the heart attack, that she would be going to the cardiac cath lab and would likely need a stent (a drug-coated device inserted in the coronary arteries to open the blockage) and that all of this would be occurring quite rapidly. Suddenly, that feeling I had earlier reared its ugly head. At 10:26 a.m., Ellen became unresponsive and her heart rhythm changed to ventricular fibrillation, a chaotic electrical pattern that causes the heart to stop, and if untreated, is fatal. I performed a precordial thump to try to terminate the rhythm, to no avail. The nurses in the room called out to the desk for help. Dr. Greg Jones, one of my associates, came into the room just as we defibrillated (electrically shocked) Ellen. Her heart rate reverted back to a normal sinus rhythm, and she regained consciousness.

At 10:58 a.m., she was taken to the cardiac cath lab. She received a stent in one vessel, and was discharged home three days later.

Ellen called me sometime in early October 2010 and told me she had been writing a book about her experience that day and asked me if I would like to contribute to it. She has been a champion of early recognition of cardiac risk factors and heart disease in women, encouraging everyone she knows to listen to her experience and learn from it. As I pondered what I would write for Ellen's book, I felt the best way to honor her ongoing efforts would be to simply tell the story in a chronological fashion, as it happened that day. She arrived at 10:08 a.m., experienced a cardiac arrest 18 minutes later, and was resuscitated within 30 seconds. She was in the cardiac cath lab 30 minutes later. This type of scenario could not be planned better -- all of the people and resources needed were in the right place at the right time. Our emergency department is a coordinated team effort whose goal is to get a patient with a myocardial infarction to the cardiac cath lab in 60 minutes or less, a goal we take very seriously.

I have thought about Ellen's case many times over the past few years, realizing how lucky she was that her arrest happened in the emergency department, where we had everything available to save her. A delay of just 5 or 10 minutes could have been the difference between life and death.

When Ellen called me about writing something for her book, I told her that I firmly believe that things happen for a reason, that each of us has a purpose in life. Clearly that was the case the day I met Ellen. When patients and families ask me what my proudest accomplishment is as an emergency medicine physician, I tell them "April 27, 2008. That day started out as a perfect day, and ended the same way." Just ask Ellen Abramson.

Chapter 2 - Who Am I?

I am Ellen Abramson and I am you. I am 53 years young and the daughter of Cookie and Edwin Epstein. I am privileged to have very supportive and wonderful parents who are excellent role models for leading a healthy lifestyle. At this stage in my life, most of my friends are taking care of their aging parents. However, due to their active lifestyle, my parents are so healthy that they were able to take care of me in my time of need.

I am married to a wonderful man, Ernest Abramson. I am grateful that he was so patient and attentive to all my needs as I worked to regain my health. He is also very supportive of my mission to spread the message about women's heart health. Together, Ernest and I have three wonderful children. Heather is 29, beautiful, brilliant, thoughtful, lovable and number one in her sales company. She recently got married to a wonderful man, a respected cardiologist named Alan. We have two handsome young sons. Eric is 26, funny, charming and loving. In his third year of law school, he is at the top of his class. Alex is 24, very humorous, in addition to being patriotic, compassionate and hard working. He just completed his fourth year of college and is looking for that "perfect job." I should not forget to mention my four-legged daughter Coco. She is an adorable, spoiled brat.

I am a motivational speaker for a large weight loss company. That has been my profession for most of my adult life, and I love it. I am very much a people person. I enjoy shopping, working out, gardening and volunteering with Go Red for Women, an organization created by the American Heart Association to raise awareness of heart disease in women. My husband and I love to visit Mexico and enjoy their rich culture. It is our dream to one day have a home there. My next big task is to master the Spanish language.

So, who am I? I am a daughter, sister, wife, mom, mother-in-law, aunt, friend, co-worker, mentor and an aspiring grandmother. It's exciting for me to say that I'm now an author. I am a woman loving life. **I am you.**

Chapter 3 - Why Write a Book?

One in Three Women Die From Heart Disease And It Could Easily be You.

Simply put, I wrote this book so you don't make the same mistakes I did. I definitely have no medical background. Talk of medical detail often makes me queasy. I'm writing this because as a survivor of cardiac arrest, I want to share my story. I am one lucky lady! Because of my good fortune, I am on a mission. That mission is to educate and spread the word that more women die of cardiovascular disease than the next five causes of death combined, including all forms of cancer. Cardiovascular disease kills approximately 460,000 women each year, which is about one death every minute. Sadly, only one in five women believes that heart disease is her greatest health threat. If I had understood that heart disease was the biggest threat to my health, it is likely that I would never have experienced cardiac arrest.

Heart disease is largely preventable. That is my message to

all women. We have the power to greatly reduce the risks of heart disease. **Only when women understand that heart disease is their greatest health threat can these horrific statistics change.** Please recognize this, and help me by spreading the word to all the women you love.

The American Heart Association started a television campaign about five years ago to inform women that heart disease is their biggest health risk. I remember watching one commercial in particular. A woman approximately my age was grieving the loss of her sister. Her message was that her sister never missed a mammogram, yet she died of heart disease. I thought to myself that I had never missed a mammogram in the past ten years or more, but I had missed many years of checkups with my family practitioner. Heart disease runs rampant in my family, however not one person has a history of breast cancer. I'm wary of breast cancer. I see women walk around without hair, an effect of their chemotherapy treatments. Evidence of breast cancer awareness is so visible. Pink ribbons are everywhere. The word is out; women constantly talk about breast cancer and mammograms. Due to fear and worry concerning breast cancer from media education, I never once missed a mammogram after my fortieth birthday. The Susan G. Komen for the Cure Foundation has done an amazing job of educating women about breast cancer. At the time I saw the above-mentioned American Heart Association commercial, I was probably in my late forties. By that time, my maternal grandfather had died at age 62 of a heart attack. My paternal grandfather had a heart attack at 50, but he lived until his second attack at age 61. My father had bypass surgery at the age of 49. I could see a pattern in the members of my family who suffered from heart disease—they were all males. I barely considered my own heart health, instead I focused my concern on my brothers.

Yes, I am a worrier. I was so naïve, I did not even know that heart disease should be on my list of worries. I soon learned that heart disease is not just a man's disease. Women lack education in this area. The common assumption is that heart disease is largely a male health issue. I was recently informed at a heart talk that more women suffer from heart attacks than men. Even as a worrier, it never once occurred to me that my life could end so quickly from a heart attack at a young age. As a worrier I should have had regular examinations with a family practitioner. If I was proactive with my heart health, I would have been informed of my heart health risks. When my symptoms began, my personal medical doctor would have guided me through the precautions needed to eliminate the events that occurred on April 27, 2008. The Heart Association tried to warn me, but I went on to learn the hard way. My hope is to make learning the lesson about heart health easier for others than it was for me. If you experience a heart attack, your outcome may not be as lucky as mine.

When women start having discussions about heart disease and prevention like we do about breast cancer and mammograms, then—and only then—can we make great strides in reducing heart disease deaths in women. One in 29 women die from breast cancer, yet one out of three die from heart disease. Please assist me and Go Red for Women of the American Heart Association in an effort to make red dresses a sight as frequent as the pink ribbons of the American Cancer Society. Working together, we can change that last statistic. Most importantly, help yourself so that you are not included in the vast number of women who suffer and die from heart disease.

Chapter 4 - My Story

For most of my life I was a very healthy eater, watching my calories closely. I lost 20 pounds when I was approximately 20 years of age. Although my weight has fluctuated throughout the years, I have kept off most of the 20 pounds. Weight maintenance is expected from me professionally, being employed by a weight loss company.

Yet at one point in my life, I had a sudden weight gain of approximately 14 pounds in four or five months. Depleted of my usual energy, I would come home from work and lie on the couch. Even the word "exhausted" seems inadequate to describe how I had felt. I became a couch potato. Anyone acquainted with me knows that normally, those words do not accurately describe me. A better adjective would be "active." I could be found in gyms and on community paths, walking and jogging. I even earned the nickname "Stairmaster Lady" at my gym. After my sudden weight gain, I tried to work out. Attempts to use the Stairmaster, treadmill and elliptical were made, but they would only last a few minutes before I headed back to the couch. My stomach often hurt. I thought it was heartburn. I felt especially sick when I drank coffee, which I had very much enjoyed. Once when I was walking up steps, my daughter complained that I was breathing heavily. I realized that something was horribly wrong.

Instead of going to my general practitioner for a physical, I popped in to a "doc-in-the-box" and complained of being tired and having constant heartburn. The doctor told me that I was getting older and needed to slow down. He handed me some over-the-counter antacid medication. But my age was not the root of my health complaints. It wasn't about slowing down. There was much more to the story and deep down, I knew it. Yet I didn't pursue the matter, because his answer wasn't scary. Ignorance was bliss, or so I thought.

On April 26th 2008, I was shopping at the local grocery store. It was Saturday night and I was buying my daughter's birthday cake. I remember feeling confused and lethargic. I saw a client and couldn't remember who she was. That was not like me and I found it bothersome. Something wasn't right.

The next day, Sunday April 27th, I died at the age of 51. I woke up early and the sun was shining. It was the first night that I had slept well in a long time. The alarm went off at seven and I jumped up, just like old times. I was happy to feel the energy that I had been missing in the previous months. With a smile on my face I began planning my day, while enjoying several cups of coffee. I did not intend it to be a typical lazy Sunday morning, as I had much to do. Our family planned to attend a St. Louis Cardinals baseball game and then go out to dinner to celebrate my daughter's 27th birthday. As an organized person, I typically have a timeline for my daily activities. That day was no different. I planned to get some gardening done, prepare for my work week and since I felt energetic, I was going to jog. I made it clear to my husband that I wanted to use the treadmill before him. Although I could have jogged outside, for some reason I opted to use the treadmill. Thank God I did, because my impulse to use the treadmill saved my life.

Playing in the muddy garden was especially fun that morning, but I had to stay on schedule. Around nine o'clock, I descended the basement steps and I heard the treadmill motor running. To my dismay, my husband was already on the treadmill and he had only been on for five minutes. Fuming, I thought this turn of events would ruin my schedule for the day. I stomped loudly up the stairs in disapproval and began to prepare for my work week.

I was contemplating the weekly discussion topic for work and sending email when all of a sudden I grabbed my chest. My left arm gyrated strangely. I immediately thought that I was having a heart attack but didn't want to believe it. I had chest pain, though I can't remember exactly what the pain felt like. Trying to lie down on the couch where I had been hanging for the past few months, I couldn't get comfortable.

I got up and walked to the basement door, flicking the lights off and on to try to get my husband's attention. My sinking feeling was that he would ignore this, thinking I did it out of anger that he was on the treadmill. I knew if I didn't get help quickly that I would have to dial 911. I went to my bathroom and called for help through the floor vent, which was positioned directly over the treadmill. Within a minute, my husband and daughter were at my side. I told them that I thought I was having a heart attack.

After a few minutes of discussion, I began to sweat profusely. There was a burning sensation in my chest. My husband got me antacid tablets. I could not stand them in my mouth, and quickly spit them out. We discussed whether or not I needed to go to the hospital. Once my husband and daughter came to help me, the urgent thought to call 911 faded. I had no idea how sick I was. My main worry was deciding whether or not to go to the hospital. Nobody wants to go on a false alarm. I didn't want to feel embarrassed or waste time. Although my husband has a medical background, he is known not to be overly cautious in such matters. My son often says that you could be dying and Dad would say, "Put a bandage on it and call me in the morning".

After a few minutes of talk, I decided to take a shower and then go to the emergency room. Still not grasping the severity of the situation, I felt I could not go dirty and smelly to the hospital. I had been in the garden and was sweating profusely. I remembered what my grandmother had told me about wearing clean underwear. As I walked into the bathroom, I yelled to my husband that I really wasn't in the mood to have a heart attack that day, and what's more, I really didn't have the time! He loves to tell everyone that; it is his favorite part of the heart attack story.

While pulling off my sweat pants before getting in the shower, I noticed with alarm that my feet were purple. Suddenly it struck me that my paternal grandfather passed away in my father's car because he took a shower and took precious time to find his robe before going to the hospital. I was only ten years of age when that happened and I remember that talk about his robe like it was yesterday. I was supposed to sleep over at my grandfather's house the night he died. The loss is still painful. Reflecting on his tragic mistake, I pulled up my sweats and called for my husband and daughter.

Off we went to the hospital. It was my first ride in my husband's new car. Through the car window I could see my next-door neighbor return home from her daily jog. She waved to me, but I didn't even have energy enough to wave back. I lay down in the back seat, feeling weak and unable to get comfortable.

We live only one mile from a wonderful hospital, but my daughter said that we should go to another hospital approximately 1/2 of a mile further. For some reason, I agreed with her and we drove the extra distance.

We arrived at the hospital at 10:00 a.m., approximately 40 minutes after the onset of my symptoms. Dr. Greg Beirne was just arriving for his ten o'clock shift. He opened the car door for me just like a valet service would. He was wearing his

Rams football jersey. I didn't think I could walk and he quickly got me a wheelchair. His caring attentiveness let me know I was in good hands. Despite my physical condition, I was in good spirits and was even cracking jokes. I told Dr. Beirne I thought I was having a heart attack, and told him what time the symptoms started. I added that I had been at home consulting with my dentist at that time. He looked at me like I was crazy. I neglected to mention to him that my husband is my dentist.

Once inside the hospital, a nurse took my pulse. Dr. Beirne looked at the numbers and then down at my purple hands. He told me not to worry, but his speed of actions indicated otherwise. The doctor dropped a stack of papers and wheeled me into a treatment room, calling for others to assist. He later told me that he knew how sick I was upon first glance at me in the car.

Unbelievably, I was the only patient in the emergency room at the time. I had lived in that area my entire life and had been in that emergency room with my family before. Never had I seen the department devoid of patients. Since then I have continued to ask hospital staff and others who live in the area and they, too, have never heard of that E.R. being empty.

Staff arrived immediately and I was hooked up to an electrocardiogram, commonly known as an EKG. Soon, a concerned Dr. Beirne said, "You're having a heart attack. Please calm down." Despite his concern, he was very much in control. I have since learned that the heart attack began at the first reading of the EKG. Generally, doctors have a few moments before chaos begins. I remember thinking that I was too tired to be anything but calm. However, that is not typical of me. I must admit feeling stressed in response to the diagnosis, but I was too tired to react much.

The room began to fill with more staff. A kind nurse named Mary stood by my side and talked with me throughout the morning. She continually reassured me that I would be all right. Mary will never know how much this meant to me. There was lots of commotion. I remember a female staff member saying that she got a call while she was at church, requesting that she report for work.

The flurry of medical talk and activity continued. I remember just wanting to sleep. I had a sinking feeling that meant I was dying. Nurse Mary removed my diamond earrings. I asked her to please give them to my daughter and to make sure she knew that I loved her. Mary, though aware of the dire situation, still continued to assure me that I would get to wear them again. It occurred to me that it was necessary to fight for my life, yet I pondered how to do that. I was so tired. I just thought I should not allow myself to fall asleep, as I felt that meant I would die. It took every ounce of energy I had just to think and to try to open my eyes. I began to pray to God for my life. "Please God," I chanted in my mind, "I wanted more time with my family."

I was aware of my daughter's presence in the room. I have nightmares about the horrified expression on her face and her steady stream of tears. In my 27 years with her, I have heard her sob, but never like this. My daughter was gripped with fear that she might lose her mother. It is a look that no mother should have to see on her child. Her face was wrinkled, she gasped for breath and her eyes were red and swollen. I felt that I had to live, just to take away her pain. I am crying as I write this, just remembering how upsetting it was.

My daughter witnessed the doctor shooting my body with epinephrine as I lay on the table, motionless and purple. When my body reacted to the drug, she saw me jump up and scream. I learned that later, from my husband, as I was in and out of consciousness. Instead of a birthday celebration to make my daughter smile, there was terror in her eyes as she helplessly looked on. She was so despondent that one of the first things that Dr. Beirne asked when I talked to him two years later was, "How is your daughter?"

I also saw my troubled husband, who was holding the curtain and mumbling. I thought he was saying that he loved me. I asked him later and he said that he was praying. I know it means the same thing. It is a scene that I would like to erase from my memory. I wanted to talk to my husband and daughter but I couldn't speak. Although I was in no physical pain, I was totally frustrated and sad for my family. All I wanted to do was tell them I loved them and that I was not in pain.

It was then that I went into cardiac arrest. My heart stopped beating. Technically I was dead, and the hospital staff immediately began a vigorous concerted effort to resuscitate me. At this point I felt as if I rose above my body. It was like water that evaporated on a summer day. I had vision, but not through my eyes. I felt what was going on. Even today I think of ways to explain this sensation, because it was so strange. My mother-in-law told me that it was just my mind playing tricks on me. I can assure you that it wasn't. If someone would have told me this story before my incident, I may have said the same thing. For that reason, I often skip this detail when I tell others about my experience.

My daughter continued to cry as my husband clawed at the curtain and mumbled frantically. Sponges flew and glass broke. When I later questioned my husband about the glass and sponges flying, he explained that one of the staff accidentally crashed a cart into the wall. It was a frightening and chaotic scene. From what I was told, Dr. Jones and Dr. Beirne were beating, pumping and shocking my heart. Ernie, my husband, often talks about the hum of the equipment getting louder as they turned the voltage up after a failed attempt. I saw everything in the room except for myself; I think it was because I didn't want to. I was relieved to feel removed from my body, which was purple and out of shape. I was self-conscious because the staff had cut off my clothes and I was lying on the table with nothing on.

Still feeling as if I was floating above my body, I waited for my grandparents, who had passed away. Where were they? It seemed like I was waiting forever. I felt alone and abandoned. Shouldn't they be there to meet me? I was upset and contemplating reasons why they were not there. Had something I said about Grandma Ida made her mad at me?

Unlike some accounts by others who died briefly and were revived, I heard no music and I saw no bright lights. I was just waiting.

Without even realizing that I had returned to my body, I heard a voice say, "Mrs. Abramson, we are going to do a lot of things very fast. Do you understand me?" I asked, "Do you know what happened to me?" There was a lot of talking. Eventually I heard the words "cardiac arrest."

Doctors, nurses, and my husband were running and talking feverishly next to my gurney until we arrived to the procedure room. I could hear someone in a fast and frantic pace praying beside me. Staff kept yelling for people to wait beyond the glass walls. Someone said they would constantly keep in touch via telephone. I had no idea who they were talking to at the time. I now realize that they kept my family and friends informed of my health status and what procedure or surgery needed to happen next.

I was lying on a metal table in a frigid room. Doctors and nurses were everywhere. I was having a cardiac catheterization. I was knowledgeable about this procedure for someone without any medical background, as both of my parents have been through this procedure many times. This procedure had always sounded frightening to me. When a patient is having a heart attack, the doctor uses this procedure to look for blockages in the arteries.

I was so scared. I knew that I had died and wondered if I was going to survive. I kept thinking that I needed to stay alive. My bones and chest hurt badly. Breathing was painful. Doctors and nurses constantly asked me how I was doing. I think I was in shock. The only question that I could answer was, "Mrs. Abramson, Do you smoke?" I remember yelling "No!" I was happy and enthusiastic to give that answer, as I quit six months prior.

The staff soon found the blockage and put in one stent in my mid circumflex artery. A stent is a small, flexible tube made of medical-grade metal and it is implanted into an artery like a scaffold to keep it open.[1] My stent in particular is coated with medicine to help further prevent blockage. This process seemed to go on forever. I was surprised to learn that it lasted only 30 to 40 minutes.

As I was wheeled out of the room, it was shocking to see so many people around me. My parents, my daughter, son, husband, my daughter's best friend and some of my friends were there as well. The only member of my immediate family who was missing was my youngest son, who was at college at that time. Everyone looked at me with red eyes. I felt so bad that I put the people I loved so much through such pain that I started to crack jokes. I just wanted to reassure them that I was going to be just fine, even though I wasn't convinced myself. I told my daughter's best friend, Paige, who was getting married in six weeks that I suffered a heart attack from all the stress of trying to find the perfect dress for her wedding. It was a long, difficult morning for my

[1]. http://www.americanheart.org/presenter.jhtml?identifier=4721

loved ones. I was so thankful to Dr. Groll and the hospital staff for getting me out of the procedure room and into intensive care.

Chapter 5 - My Husband's Perspective of What Happened On That Day

It happened fast. Faster than you can even imagine. In just a matter of seconds, I was escorted out of the treatment room by two nurses and was told to please sit in a wheelchair, in anticipation of what they were going to have to tell me. I already knew. The look on nurse Peg's face said it all. To my left, Heather, my daughter, was crying hysterically in the waiting room. To my right, at the end of the hall, the chaplain was pacing back and forth in an ominous black outfit. I pretended not to make eye contact. Death, it seemed, had made its presence known in no uncertain terms. Death, it appeared, was not going to be denied.

In their haste to begin CPR, the staff accidentally forgot to close the curtain, so I witnessed everything. Drs. Beirne and Jones worked feverishly on what appeared to be a motionless blue mass, that moments prior, was my wife. They worked as if there was no tomorrow, and in truth, there wasn't. Things were going from bad to worse, a total disaster.

I took a few steps back, surveyed the entire scenario again and heard the hum of the defibrillator in preparation for what was going to be one final massive electrical shock. I said nothing. I looked straight ahead and the following are the exact thoughts that went through my mind:

"If You really and truly do exist, If You are really out there and can hear my thoughts, well, I need Your help. This is very quickly turning into a funeral. What can I do? What am I going to do? So if it's true, that You really do exist, if You're really out there, then now is the time. I don't need Your help sometime in the distant future, I need it right now. So I'm asking You, please...no...I'm begging You...to please...just this once...show Yourself. Just show Yourself."

He did just that. To this day, I don't know how long I stood in that hallway. I lost all concept of time. It simply didn't exist. It may have been minutes, or hours, or maybe it didn't happen at all. It seemed surreal. To this day, I still don't know how I was able to maintain my thoughts in such a calm and organized manner. Believe me, daily occurrences that are far less significant than this one do tend to rattle me. Perhaps some other force was always in control and I didn't realize it.

Chapter 6 - Intensive Care

Once in intensive care, I was hooked up to what seemed like every medical machine known to mankind. Doctors and nurses did everything without a single complaint from me. Being alive and with my family was all that mattered. My mother was rubbing my head. The chaplain kept praying. I looked up at her and said, "Sherry, it's me, Elle." Sherry said in a startled voice, "Elle, didn't you just send me an email this morning?" I believe that I sent her an email from home at the same time I had the initial chest pain.

My stay in intensive care lasted three days. During the first two days, I didn't say or do very much. By the last day, I began to drive my nurse Sonny crazy. She awarded me the title of the "healthiest patient in intensive care." Soon she let me go to the step down and I happily relinquished my title. I was one step closer to home.

Out of intensive care, I enjoyed being attached to fewer medical devices and had the freedom to use a bathroom. Not having a

Ellen S. Abramson

catheter was major for me. I even got to walk for the first time in three days. As I recovered, I started to despise being in the hospital. I left the step down after one day. That was the first day of the rest of my life.

Chapter 7 - It Took a Few Moments Of Death To Learn How To Live

Two years have passed since this incident and it's been an incredible journey. While I definitely wouldn't recommend having a heart attack to anyone, looking back I consider the experience a gift.

Before my heart attack I attended a benefit luncheon for cancer. It was hosted by a good friend and neighbor Pamela, a very special and courageous breast cancer survivor. One of the speakers was Fran Drescher, a cancer survivor herself. She said that cancer was a "present wrapped up in an ugly package." For some reason, her words struck a chord with me and never left my head. I reflected on those words after my heart attack and they have proved to be true.

Life is different these days. My heart attack was such a wake-up call to me. I start each day by looking at a card sent to me from the hospital. The card is signed by most of the staff that saved my life. Because their excellent care enabled me to live, I feel so grateful to each and every one of them. An invitation to celebrate my 52nd birthday was sent to all who assisted in my medical care. Now, instead of dreading birthdays, I celebrate them. After reading my hospital note, I thank God and pray. Before my heart attack I would pray if I was worried about something, or just in case. Now I pray often and thank God for my life and everything in it.

In the past two years so many wonderful things have happened. Or is it that I only see wonderful things? I have had time to know my adorable son-in-law, danced at my daughter's wedding and I recently saw my son graduate from law school. Before I got sick, I doubted my friendships. My heart attack made me realize that people are wonderful and I am so blessed with friends. It is common for people to be too busy and take friendships for granted. We shouldn't do that. You never know what tomorrow may bring. As the saying goes, "Life is not a dress rehearsal." Let's stop giving lip service to ideas without practicing them. If things happen for a reason, then I believe the reason I am a cardiac arrest survivor is to help save lives through education.

I have a voice and I have chosen to use it. I need your help. If you are a woman or if you love a woman, then I am inviting you to join my team. Please tell every woman that you love that heart disease is her greatest health threat. Love yourself and start making the changes you need to be heart healthy. Maria

Robinson, a health educator said, "Nobody can go back and start a new beginning, but anyone can start today and make a new ending." Live your life and live it well. **I have learned that what your loved ones really want for their birthdays, weddings and graduations is to spend them with you.**

Chapter 8 - Oprah Didn't Call and I Didn't Care

I have always admired Oprah and it has always been a dream of mine to be on her show. A co-worker sent me a notice that Oprah was looking for women who had experienced a heart attack. My daughter, son and son-in-law wrote letters to Oprah. I thought that being on the show would be the icing on the cake. I was so wrong! Reading the letters that my children wrote was the icing on the cake and the cherry on top! Oprah didn't call and it really didn't matter. These letters that I am going to share with you are among my most prized possessions. My children's confrontation with my near death was devastating for them. As women we are the caretakers. We get busy doing everything for everyone else. We need to understand that we must take care of ourselves too. We need to be there for the people that love us.

Ellen S. Abramson

From My Daughter Heather

I am writing on the behalf of my mother, Ellen Abramson. She is a strong, intelligent and beautiful woman. I am proud to be her daughter and thank God everyday that she is alive! I watched my mother go into cardiac arrest twice the day after my 27th birthday. My family has a long line of heart disease, although the history only included the men in my family. Before her heart attack, my mother was a vibrant, active woman who worked for a weight loss company; a picture of health, not of disease. That is why that Sunday morning was a huge surprise that will haunt me for the rest of my life. I could recount the horror that occurred that day or her painful road to recovery. However, I would rather focus on the beauty of her story.

My mother was resuscitated to save lives. The first life she saved was her own. Before her heart attack she seemed to be in the all too well known rut of sleep, eat, work and laundry. Her lifestyle became rather monotonous to say the least. She now lives her life to the fullest spending her free time strengthening bonds with family and friends. Her desire to live and inspire is infectious! My mother has turned her tragic incident into a blessing. She has become very involved with the Heart Association and has been speaking and educating women on heart disease for the past two years. She has so much passion for her work and the way she is able to captivate people with her story is incredible! I remember the first time I heard her tell her story at the

Heart Association luncheon. It was actually a video that played on several large screens at the Ritz Carlton in St. Louis. I listened to her words as I replayed the horror in my head and began to cry. I was sobbing because it was my story too! However, what I didn't realize was that it was a story that could touch and empower so many. As I looked around the room there were hundreds of women sharing my same tears. My mother has a huge heart, a strong voice and a story that can change lives.

Ellen S. Abramson

From My Son-in-Law Alan

Heart disease is my life! My grandfather died of a heart attack at age 52, and I became the third generation Cardiologist in my family. I work with cardiac patients on a daily basis, yet I never thought I would marry into a family as involved in heart disease as my wife's. Ellen Abramson, my new mother-in-law, was 51 years old. She exercised, maintained her weight, and felt healthy, until one morning she awoke with a suffocating sensation. She was rushed to the Emergency Department where she collapsed minutes after arriving. She was resuscitated and sent to the cathlab where her coronary artery was stented. Since the day she began cardiac rehab two and a half years ago, Ellen has answered a calling: to make people aware of the previlence of heart disease in women. She volunteers her free time to the American Heart Association's Go Red campaign, disseminating information about her experience, creating a conscience about this silent killer within our community. She uses her podium to promote an active lifestyle, weight and blood pressure control, and health improvement in order to minimize the impact of heart disease one person at a time. She is a truly gifted speaker who connects with anyone who listens, as her life is real and her situation is becoming more common in our world. Ellen would be a great asset to your show, she has a story to share, that is fortunately accompanied by a happy ending that continues. The link to her story can be found in

    http://www.youtube.com/watch?v=qtQMI7I4MEw <http://www.youtube.com/watch?v=qtQMI7I4MEw>

From My Son Eric

As I had awakened on that tragic morning, instant confusion arose. I heard my father informing me that my mother was being rushed to the hospital. He wasn't sure what was wrong. When I heard the urgency in my mother's voice, I knew it was best for me to hurry to the hospital to check on my mother. Instantly upon my arrival, my father told me that everything was under control, that my mother was fine, and to go back home and make sure I closed the garage door. I went home and closed the door at my father's request. Upon returning to the emergency room for the second time that morning, I witnessed my mother's bed being rushed into the elevator on the way to the operating room. I have never felt so shocked and afraid in my life. I got into the elevator with my mother and the physicians, and I could hardly get a word out. My mother looked up at me and told me she was fine, although this obviously was not the case. Before I knew it, the worst had become a reality. I was told that my mother had suffered a Myocardial Infarction, and was in need of a prompt surgical procedure. All I could do is wait and hope for the best. I will never forget the morning I almost lost the most important woman in my life.

Go Red Event February 2009 -

From left to right: Sister-in-law Amy, daughter Heather, Ellen, friends Debbie and Lori.

May 2010-Ellen with husband Ernie in Mexico City.

September 3, 2010- Ellen's two handsome sons Eric and Alex.

September 4, 2010- Ellen's daughter Heather with her new husband Alan.

September 4, 2010-Ellen's parents Cookie and Ed with bride and groom.

September 3, 2010-Ellen, Heather, Ernie and Mother-in-law Elaine

May, 2011- Eric's law school graduation in Orlando, Florida.

Part Two
What Are You Willing To Do?

What are you willing to do so that you are NOT among the one out of three women who will die from heart disease?

If I were you, I would not gamble. The odds are not in your favor.

Chapter 9 - A Few Lines from Ralph Marston, a Favorite Poet of Mine

Forget the excuses, let go of the should, move beyond the if onlys, and ask yourself this one question. Are you willing or are you not? All the many things that go into any achievement can be reduced to one clear and simple factor. And that is-Are you willing?

When you are willing to do what it takes, you will find a way. When you are willing, though circumstances conspire against you, you'll get it done anyway.

> Somewhere, somehow, there is something that will inspire and engage you fully. Connect yourself with it and suddenly, you'll be willing, willing to do whatever it takes.
>
> *Ralph Marston*

Chapter 10 - Heart Disease is Highly Preventable

I find it important to list the lifestyle choices I made prior to my heart attack that may have affected my heart health.

NOT TO LECTURE YOU BUT...PLEASE DO NOT SMOKE

I began smoking when I was a teen. I guess it made me feel cool. I soon became addicted to cigarettes. As we all do, I have several regrets in life. However, if granted one "do-over", it would be to never, put one cigarette to my lips.

Smoking wasn't a good fit for my lifestyle. I am a mother, an exercise enthusiast and a motivational speaker for a weight loss company. I am also an intelligent woman who understood the risks of smoking. Due to my embarrassment about being a smoker, I went to great lengths to hide my habit. I am not sure if I was fooling anyone but myself. I continued to smoke because I was afraid of gaining weight and didn't want to go through the withdrawal period. The truth is that the fantasy of the withdrawal period was more of a monster in my mind than it actually was. Just like everything else, it was mind over matter. The reality is that I enjoyed smoking. I guess my addiction was stronger than the embarrassment and the fear of health problems.

If I had only known then what I know now. My family had begged me to quit. Six months before my heart attack, my friend Jessica told me she quit. She told me about auricular therapy. Auricular therapy is the electrical stimulation of multiple acupuncture points in the ear. Proponents of the therapy claim that it helps minimize cravings while strengthening willpower. I had tried the therapy once before, yet upon leaving the office I had a cigarette. I was hoping for a magical cure. Jessica told me that auricular therapy was helpful. Something about what she said made me listen. So I tried auricular therapy for a second time. Soon my desire to quit overcame my desire to smoke. "Nothing will work unless you do." Quotation attributed to John Wooden, American basketball coach, and Maya Angelou, American Writer.

When people are sick, they tend to watch a lot of television. Home from the hospital and recovering, I watched a celebrity drug rehabilitation show with Dr. Drew. One of the counselors said something to the effect of, how many years do we use drugs to avoid three weeks of withdrawal? He said it all; if I was able to quit smoking, anyone can. You just have to make up your mind. Smoking is a major risk factor for heart disease. Your heart health improves within minutes of quitting. "Twenty

Live to Dance

minutes after quitting your heart rate and blood pressure will drop. Twelve hours after quitting the carbon monoxide level in your blood falls to normal and three weeks to three months after quitting your circulation and lung function improve[2]." "After one year, your heart diseases risk is cut in half. After ten years of not smoking, your heart disease risk is the same as someone who has never smoked".[3] Before I completely quit smoking, I spent years reducing the number of cigarettes I smoked. I found that continually making an effort to reduce the number of cigarettes smoked made it easier for me to give them up altogether.

---

2. http://health.msn.com/health-topics/quit-smoking/articlepage.aspx?cp-documentid=100226450
3. www.CDC.gov/tobacco/sgr

Chapter 11 - Being Proactive

It is important for people to have a physical each and every year. A twelve-year-old client much wiser than her years told me after my attack, "The doctor is your friend." Do research on your medical professionals before you select them. Aside from professional expertise, it is important that your doctor pays attention and devotes enough time to address your questions and concerns. A good doctor will listen to you and ask you specific questions about your health history. Stay informed about your health risks and make sure to communicate them with your doctor. A good doctor will help you to develop a plan to manage your risk factors.

The Go Red for Women organization stresses the importance of patients knowing and understanding their "numbers." In striving for heart health, the numbers to know are: blood pressure, cholesterol, fasting blood glucose, triglycerides, body mass index, waist circumference, minutes of activity and cigarettes per day. These figures help us to understand our cardiovascular risks.

Make sure all of your doctors work as a team. Once you have excellent health care, continue to be proactive. If you feel that something is wrong with your health, it's very important to trust your instincts and find answers. Don't take no for an answer. If your doctor does not listen or act upon your health concerns, perhaps it's time to make a change.

Chapter 12 - Act Quickly

When I had my heart attack, I learned the important lesson about how to react to the onset of symptoms. I learned not to waste precious time debating with family about whether to go to the hospital. Whatever is keeping you from going to the hospital-whether it is indecision, denial, fear, or even superficial concerns like showering or changing clothes-drop everything and get medical help immediately. Do not get into a car. If no family or friends are there to call for help on your behalf, call 911 and lie by the front door with it unlocked in case you pass out.

Doctors will advise patients about medical alert systems, jewelry identifications and medication lists along with doctor names and numbers to be carried in your wallet. Medical staff is trained to look for such identifications. Immediate medical treatment can limit damage to your heart or brain. I was lucky to be at the hospital when my arrest occurred. If it happened in the car, the outcome would have been different. Medical staff and equipment are necessary to save your life. Do not count on luck.

Chapter 13 - Be Aware of the Warning Signs

Some symptoms of heart attack include: chest discomfort, back or shoulder blade or jaw pain in women. Many women experience different pain than men. Often women do not report chest discomfort. Do not let the absence of chest pain keep you from heading to the Emergency Room. Other symptoms are: discomfort in other areas of the upper body, shortness of breath, cold sweat, nausea or dizziness, fatigue or weakness or sense of impending doom.

CHAPTER 14 - KNOW YOUR NUMBERS

Factor	Goal	
Total Cholesterol	Less than 200 mg/dL	
LDL ("Bad") Cholesterol	LDL cholesterol goals vary.	
	Less than 100 mg/dL	Optimal
	100 to 129 mg/dL	Near Optimal/Above Optimal
	130 to 159 mg/dL	Borderline High
	160 to 189 mg/dL	High
	190 mg/dL and above	Very High
HDL ("Good") Cholesterol	50 mg/dL or higher	
Triglycerides	<150 mg/dL	
Blood Pressure	<120/80 mmHg	
Fasting Glucose	<100 mg/dL	
Body Mass Index (BMI)	<25 Kg/m²	
Waist Circumference	<35 inches	
Exercise	Minimum of 30 minutes most days, if not all days of the week	

* "<" means "less than"

Reprinted with permission
www.goredforwomen.org
©2011, American Heart Association, Inc.

Healthy Weight Ranges

Height	BMI=20	BMI=25
5' 0"	95	125
5' 1"	100	125
5' 2"	105	130
5' 3"	105	135
5' 4"	110	140
5' 5"	110	145
5' 6"	110	150
5' 7"	115	155
5' 8"	125	160
5' 9"	130	168
5' 10"	130	170
5' 11"	135	175
6' 0"	140	180
6' 1"	145	185
6' 2"	145	190
6' 3"	150	195

NOTE: 20 to 25 is the healthy range.

Chapter 15 - The Two Things That I Did Right

EAT RIGHT AND GET YOUR WEIGHT INTO A HEALTHY BODY MASS INDEX FOR GOOD HEART HEALTH

"People who are overweight are more likely to develop heart disease even if they have no other risk factors. Obesity is unhealthy because excess weight puts more strain on your heart. You can reduce your risk of heart disease by reaching and staying at your best weight. That means cutting back on fats and eating more fruits, vegetables and grains. It also means being physically active."

Quotation attributed to the American Heart Association.

I believe what you put in your body and what you do with it will determine either your best or worst health. Julius Erving, a famous pro basketball player, said, "If you don't do what's best for your body, you're the one who comes up on the short end." I believe in clean eating. We are what we eat.

Most of the time I eat non-processed foods. Non-processed foods are foods that grow on the farm, roam the land or swim in the water. I always tell my clients, there should be no hot dogs on your farm. Your farm animals should only have one mother. These foods are rich in vitamins and are very filling as they are full of water, air and fiber. For optimal heart health choose olive oil when cooking and make sure to limit saturated and trans fats.

You should not deprive yourself of higher calorie foods that do not grow on the farm. It's all about moderation. Make good choices most of the time. Deprivation can lead to binging and low-self esteem. I believe in the 85-15 rule. If 85 percent of the time you are eating clean non processed foods then 15 percent of the time you can enjoy some other food. If I could only say one thing about weight loss, it would be that diets do not work. Diets are about deprivation and have endings.

Losing weight is a lifestyle change of behaviors that made you overweight in the first place. Once those behaviors are identified then you can learn how to replace them with healthier ones. Basically, it means to learn the eating behaviors of a thin person. This type of weight loss is not quick and effortless. It requires a lot of work and commitment but the weight loss is healthy, sustainable and worth it. In simple terms, weight loss means to eat less and move more. I know you can do it.

Live to Dance

How Do I Begin to Lose Weight?

Believe in Yourself. Know you can accomplish your goals.

"If you think you can or can't, you're right."

Henry Ford

Chapter 16 - How Do I Begin to Lose Weight?

While the concept of weight loss is simple, getting started can be overwhelming and lead to procrastination. The best time to **start** is **now**. "You can't get much done by starting tomorrow." Not on Monday, when finals are over, when the children are out of school and certainly not after vacation.

Begin by making a list of all the reasons you want to lose weight. Examples on your list may be: to fight heart disease, reduce blood pressure, fit into clothing, improve self-esteem, be a good role model for children, be able to easily fit on an airplane seat or a carnival ride. Keep this list accessible at all times. Many times we give up on weight loss for the sole reason that we forget what we want most because of what is sitting in front of us.

Support

Find a weight loss group for **support**. The weight loss journey will have many ups and downs. You will have some turbulent times. During these times, the support group will help you to understand that you are not alone. This setting will provide you with others who are going through the same struggles. You will be able to share your feelings without worry of shame or criticism. Members will be sympathetic and understanding when it comes to your pitfalls, fears and concerns. They will lend an ear and offer advice. The group can often coach members to stay the course. The real measure of success is how you will handle difficult times. Recovery is everything.

Most importantly, group support offers hope and confidence that you will achieve your goals. You will experience and see the success of others. The group will help you to celebrate your own success and get you to the healthy weight goal that you deserve.

Clean Your Environment

Get rid of all junk or trigger foods. Clear out your pantry, refrigerator, desk drawers and your car. It would be difficult to lose weight if your environment is littered with high calorie foods. High calorie or "sometimes food" are best enjoyed out of your personal space. It is easier to enjoy one piece of cake at a restaurant than at home with ten other pieces calling your name.

Shop

Fill your refrigerator with fruits, vegetables, low-fat dairy and lean proteins. These foods will make weight loss easier. You will eat what is available.

Start Setting Goals

Everyone who is successful is **goal** oriented. A goal will help to give you direction. When the big picture feels overwhelming, small goals will help give you motivation to concentrate your efforts on one specific task. They will also help you to celebrate progress and help foster that "I can attitude" that is crucial for success.

The trick is to learn how to set goals. Goals need to be specific, measurable, attainable, stated in the positive and behaviorally based. Instead of saying, "I will exercise this week", say "I will walk three times this week for a total of sixty minutes." It is specific, measurable and stated in the positive. This goal clearly states what you want to do. Attainable means a good fit with your life. If you have never walked before, 60 minutes may be doable. Do not set yourself up for failure by making a goal of running a marathon the first week you begin.

Goals need to be behaviorally based. The behaviors of exercise, journaling meals and eating while seated at the table will get you the weight loss you are looking for. For example, "I will lose three pounds this week" may set you up for failure. Numbers of pounds per week are not always within your control; behaviors are.

Work on small changes. Small changes can make a big difference over the long term. Make an exercise and an eating goal each and every week. Note: Weight loss tips in the following section will be helpful when setting behavioral goals.

"If you bite it, write it." **Journaling** is the universal key to weight loss. Keeping track of everything you eat makes you accountable and will help you to stay on track. Mindless eating is the enemy. I personally had a condition that I diagnosed as food amnesia. No permanent cure can be found for this condition. It is only managed through journaling much like diseases that can be managed with medications. Not only should you track what you eat, but also the portion size of what you eat.

Have a Conversation with a Medical Doctor or Nutritionist

When all is said and done, losing weight is a simple mathematical formula. You need to burn more than you eat to lose weight. If you eat 500 calories less than you burn, it is probable that you will lose a healthy weight loss of one to two pounds a week. To lose a pound of fat you must burn 3,500 calories.

You have a few options. Ask a medical doctor or a nutritionist how many calories you need to consume per day to lose weight healthily. You can also enlist in a reputable support group with a healthy weight loss system in place.

CHAPTER 17 - WEIGHT LOSS TIPS

TO GET YOUR BODY INTO A HEALTHY BODY MASS INDEX (BMI)

Grocery Store

1. Do not go to the grocery store hungry.
2. Make a list before you go and stick to it.
3. Do not buy groceries in bulk or excess. I like to buy individual serving sizes.
4. Shop mostly in the perimeter of the grocery store for filling or non-processed foods.
5. Wear tight clothing when shopping to help make good food choices.

Dining Out

1. Plan ahead. Menus and nutritional facts can often be found on the internet. If you plan on consuming excessive calories, work out more and eat lower calorie foods that day. But be sure to follow tip number 2.
2. Do not go out to eat starving. Eat an apple or a filling food so that you do not attack high calorie breads and appetizers. Not being overly hungry will help you make good choices when ordering. Note: Free bread is not free; you will pay for it later.
3. Limit alcoholic beverages. Restaurants know that customers who drink more, order and eat more. Not to mention that alcoholic beverages have calories.
4. Order first so that you will not be persuaded by what others order.
5. Order broth base soups or salads to fill up on first.
6. Ask questions about preparations. Go for words like broiled, baked, grilled, steamed or poached. Beware of food preparations described as augratin, parmigiana, tempura, alfredo, creamy and carbonara.
7. Ask for salad dressings and sauces on the side. Dip your fork into the dressing instead of pouring dressing over the salad.
8. If you like desserts, look at the dessert menu first. If you choose to order one, go light on the main dish.
9. Thin people do not dine at buffets!
10. Do not dine with old "eating buddies".

Portion Control at Restaurants

1. Take half of the dinner home in a "doggy bag." Ask the server to wrap up half the dinner before even serving.
2. Split your dinner with a friend.
3. If ordering a dinner high in calories, order from the appetizer list to help with portion control.
4. A serving of protein should be approximately the size of your palm minus your fingers. (3 ounces) One serving of pasta should be the size of your fist. (one cup)
5. If you do go to a buffet; choose to eat off of a salad plate.
6. If you choose a dinner plate; arrange your food by three o'clock. Between the twelve and the three place your protein. Between the three and six place a carbohydrate and between the six and twelve place vegetables. Start your meal with the vegetables.

Home

1. Eat only when seated at the table.
2. Keep a "clean" environment. Do not keep junk food in your house. It is difficult to behave in an environment littered with junk food.
3. Load up your kitchen with healthy non-processed foods. You will eat what's available.
4. Do not linger in the kitchen.
5. Do not take food to the couch or bed.
6. Do not multi-task while eating.

Portion Control at Home

1. Eat off of small plates.
2. Arrange food on your plate three o'clock style. Place protein between the twelve and three. Place starch between the three and six and vegetables between the six and twelve.
3. Eat ice cream or cereal in coffee mugs.
4. Do not serve buffet style.
5. Make cakes and meat loafs in muffin tins for portion control. If a cake yields twelve servings, bake in twelve muffin tins.
6. Do not eat snacks out of bags unless they are single servings.

General

1. Chew your food. Eat slowly and enjoy every bite.
2. Put your fork down between bites. Remember, the fork is not a shovel!
3. If you have company, talk between bites. Enjoy your company more than your food.
4. Ask yourself, what am I hungry for? "If hunger is not the question, then food is not the answer."
5. Do not subscribe to the "clean plate club."
6. Stop eating when full, even if it is your favorite food.
7. "If you bite it, write it." Journal everything you eat. Remember, what you eat in private, you wear in public.
8. Keep healthy snacks in your car, your purse or brief case just in case.
9. Do not weigh yourself daily. Daily weigh-ins can lead to frustration.
10. Ease up on weight-loss expectations. An average of a pound per week is awesome.
11. Successful people set goals. Make sure they are specific and are realistic.

Work

1. Bring your lunch when possible.
2. Do not linger in the staff lounge if it is littered with junk foods.
3. Use the steps at work.
4. Eat a healthy snack in the car on the way home from work so that you do not raid the pantry before dinner.

Friends and Family

1. Ask for what you need.
2. Know who to ask for what. Understand that some people will not be willing to help you.
3. Find a support group or a weight loss buddy.
4. I dare you to make plans that do not have anything to do with food.

Closet

1. Get rid of clothes that are too large. Large clothing makes it easy when you gain weight.
2. Keep trying on clothes that almost fit. It will help further progress.

Chapter 18 - Exercise

Exercise Benefits

For most of the past 25 years I have exercised six out of seven days. I enjoy exercising. While I do not wake up and chant the words exercise, I do love how it makes me feel. Aerobics not only burns calories but it takes away worries and gives me more energy while enabling me to sleep better at night. I have always liked the phrase, "Use it or lose it." I enjoy walking and jogging to music, using the Stairmaster, the Elliptical, weight training, spinning bikes and swimming. Aerobics are the way I start my day. It is a part of my lifestyle. I know a lot about exercise and the many health advantages that exercise can offer. I talk about it often in my meetings:

1. General heart health. The heart increases its blood stroke volume.
2. Resting heart rate slows.
3. Oxygen is used more efficiently.
4. More energy in the day.
5. Better sleep at night.
6. Increased endurance.

7. Lowers blood pressure.
8. Reduces risks in developing diabetes and most other diseases including certain cancers and osteoporosis.
9. Increases good cholesterol.
10. Decreases bad cholesterol.
11. More efficient cardiovascular system.
12. Better chance of maintaining weight.
13. Helps to burn calories.
14. Increases flexibility and mobility.
15. Improves memory.
16. Reduces anxiety and depression. Builds confidence and an "I can" attitude.

But I never heard of Number 17 and that would be collateral circulation. Number 17 saved my life. The hospital cardiologist noticed on my x-ray that I was an avid exerciser. Wow! I never knew that exercising would show up on a heart x-ray.

"Collateral circulation" refers to the development of new branches of blood vessels in response to exercise. Regular vigorous aerobic exercise may stimulate the formation of the new branches of the coronary arteries. This may offset the effects of a thrombosis (clot). If one of the coronary arteries becomes blocked, the new vessels can provide the blood with an alternative pathway to maintain the supply of oxygen and nutrients to the heart. Good collateral circulation may also accelerate the recovery from a heart attack[4]. That must be the reason for cardiac rehabilitation. The doctor felt that this was the big reason I was revived. I can also give credit to excellent doctors and some good luck. I am happy to tell you that I have no heart damage. I have a perfect heart.

---

4. http://www.americanheart.org/presenter.jhtml?identifier=4583

Exercise Tips

Plan for it. Enter exercise on your calendar much like any other appointment.

Experiment. Find an activity you like to do. Try to do what you liked when you were younger. Maybe biking, basketball, or even jump rope.

If you like music, then enjoy music while walking or working out in the gym.

Park your car further from your destination.

Use steps instead of elevators and escalators when safe.

Wear a pedometer. It will challenge you to walk more each day. It is suggested that you should walk 10,000 steps each day. Ten thousand steps equals five miles.

Make social plans that involve activity.

Chapter 19 - Five Key Take-Aways From Your Local Cardiologist:

1. Control your cholesterol. Cholesterol begins to deposit in the arteries that feed the heart late by age 20, originating plaques of atherosclerosis causing blockages. High cholesterol and LDL increase the rate of deposit, increasing the risk of a heart attack or stroke. High cholesterol may be a reflection of diet or of inherited factors. Exercise and diet are the first steps that need to be taken to keep the cholesterol under control. If these efforts are not enough, then taking a cholesterol lowering pill is recommended. According to the United States Protective Services Task Force, cholesterol screening should be initiated in men after the age of 35 or women after 45 years of age. Screening and treatment should be started earlier in anyone who has a strong family history of heart disease.
2. Control your blood pressure. High blood pressure has been linked to heart attacks, strokes, kidney and heart failure. By being proactive and lowering blood pressure to 130/80 mmHg (in patients with diabetes or kidney problems) or < 140/90 mmHg, the risk of having a heart attack drops by a fourth, strokes by one third, and heart failure by a half.[5]

---

5. Chobanian AV, Bakris GL, Black HR, Cushman WC, Green LA, et al. The Seventh Report of the Joint National Committee on Prevention, Detection, Evaluation, and Treatment of High Blood Pressure : the JNC 7 report. JAMA 2003;289:2560-72.

3. Control your blood sugar. Diabetes is very common, and has grave consequences if not treated seriously. A quarter of patients with diabetes will have blockages of the arteries that feed the heart. People with diabetes have the same risk of dying from heart disease than those who have 3 risk factors (high blood pressure, high cholesterol, and smoking).[6] People with diabetes have the same risk of having a heart attack than non-diabetic people who have already had one.[7] Strict control of blood glucose is extremely important in preventing the developments of coronary artery disease.
4. Control your weight and watch what you eat. The rate of obesity has been increasing at an alarming rate in the United States and affects people of all ages. Obesity correlates with the growing number of diabetics as well. Being overweight limits physical activity due to joint pains, which then promote more physical de-conditioning leading to a spiral of worsening inactivity. Weight loss is recommended for everyone who is overweight. Physical activity and behavior modification to achieve and maintain weight loss is crucial. Moderate weight loss is associated with improvement in all the factors that are associated with heart disease: blood pressure, blood glucose, triglycerides and total cholesterol.[8] Type 2 diabetes can be prevented by controlling weight and simple lifestyle modifications in patients who are overweight.[9] Limiting the level of saturated fats to 7% of all dietary intake with minimal consumption of transfat will help achieve this.
5. Be active. High activity level is a simple way of keeping

---

6. UKPDS Investigators. Intensive glucose control with sulphonylureas or insulin compared with conventional treatment and risk of complications in patients with type 2 diabetes. Lancet 1998; 352:837.
7. Haffner, SM, Lehto S, Ronnemaa T, Pyorala K, Laakso M. Mortality from coronary heart disease in subjects with Type 2 diabetes and in nondiabetic subjects with and without prior myocardial infarction. N Engl J Med 1998;339:229-234.
8. Case CC, Jones PH, Nelson K, O'Brian SE, Ballantyne CM. Impact of Weight loss on the metabolic syndrome. *Diabetes Obes Metab.* 2002;4:407-414.
9. Knowler WC, Barrett-Connor E, Fowler SE, Hamman RF, Lachin JM, et al. Reduction in the incidence of type 2 diabetes with lifestyle intervention or metformin. N Engl J Med 2002;346:393-403.

healthy. Brisk walking with a goal of 10,000 steps per day is ideal for patients without orthopedic problems that may limit their mobility. Using a pedometer to monitor daily steps is easy. Having a step goal is an easy way to monitor improvement in physical activity. Water exercises are a great option for people with severe joint pains or back problems.

PART THREE
Your Workbook

"The road to someday, leads to the town of nowhere. Procrastination is the silent killer."

-Anthony Robbins

Top Ten Reasons I want to Live

I began to pray for my life. Please God, I chanted in my mind, I want more time with my family.

Ellen Abramson

1. _____
2. _____
3. _____
4. _____
5. _____
6. _____
7. _____
8. _____
9. _____
10. _____

Goals

"The reason most people never reach their goals is that they don't define them, or even seriously consider them as believable or achievable. Winners can tell you where they are going, what they plan to do along the way, and who will be sharing the adventure with them."

Denis Watley

_____
_____
_____
_____
_____
_____
_____
_____
_____
_____
_____
_____
_____
_____

Food & Exercise Journal

Date:_____ Net Calories_____

Meal	Food	Calories

Activity	Duration	Calories

Action Steps

When the big picture feels overwhelming, small steps will help give you motivation to concentrate your efforts.

Write specific, measurable, attainable action steps stated in the positive. Make sure they are behaviorally based. Review Chapters 16 – 18 for ideas.

Examples of good action steps:

I will call the doctor's office and schedule a check up this week. Rather than…I will schedule a doctor's appointment.

I will walk twenty minutes three times this week. Rather than…I will stop being so lazy.

I will fill one half of my plate with fresh fruit and vegetables four times this week. Rather than…I will eat more fruits and vegetables.

Action Steps for Week 1

1. _____
2. _____
3. _____
4. _____
5. _____

"Celebrate what you want to see more of."

Thomas J. Peters

Successes This Week to Celebrate:

_____
_____
_____
_____
_____
_____
_____
_____
_____
_____

Action Steps for Week 2

1. _____

2. _____

3. _____

4. _____

5. _____

"Celebrate what you want to see more of."

Thomas J. Peters

Successes This Week to Celebrate:

_____
_____
_____
_____
_____
_____
_____
_____

Action Steps for Week 3

1. _____
2. _____
3. _____
4. _____
5. _____

"Celebrate what you want to see more of."

Thomas J. Peters

Successes This Week to Celebrate:

_____

Action Steps for Week 4

1. _____

2. _____

3. _____

4. _____

5. _____

"Celebrate what you want to see more of."

Thomas J. Peters

Successes This Week to Celebrate:

_____
_____
_____
_____
_____
_____
_____
_____

Action Steps for Week 5

1. _____
2. _____
3. _____
4. _____
5. _____

"Celebrate what you want to see more of."

Thomas J. Peters

Successes This Week to Celebrate:

_____
_____
_____
_____
_____
_____
_____
_____
_____

Action Steps for Week 6

1. _____
2. _____
3. _____
4. _____
5. _____

"Celebrate what you want to see more of."

Thomas J. Peters

Successes This Week to Celebrate:

_____
_____
_____
_____
_____
_____
_____
_____

And the best reason for surviving yet...

Twin grandchildren – Raquel and Leo!